Old Drogheda

Hugh Oram

A group of hardy dock workers in Drogheda port a century ago, a time when the port was bringing in shipments of coal and exporting cattle so their work would have been onerous. Cotton yarn for the local textile factories was another big import and the port had a substantial workforce of over a hundred dock labourers. In 1850, 550 sailing vessels entered the port, as well as 210 of the then new-fangled steamers. Just over 50 years later, in 1907, 254 coastal steamers used the port, while the number of coastal sailing ships had fallen to 66.

Text © Hugh Oram, 2011.
First published in the United Kingdom, 2011,
by Stenlake Publishing Ltd.
01290 551122
www.stenlake.co.uk

ISBN 9781840335606

Printed by
P2D Books, 1 Newlands Rd, Westoning, Bedford MK45 5LD

The publishers regret that they cannot supply copies of any pictures featured in this book.

Acknowledgements

I should like to thank the following people for their generous help with my enquiries: Brendan Matthews and Dr T.K. Whitaker, to both of whom I owe a special debt of gratitude; James Coogan; Betty Quinn; Johnny McLeer; Emmett Doran; Daniel Mullan; Declan Quaile; John Callan; Paul Allen; John Graeme Igoe; Paudie Wall; Malachy McCloskey; Joseph H. Downes; Peter Lyons; Bill Crimmins; Audrey Tinsley; Ceara Shearman; Joe Egan; Gregg Ryan; Mark Nulty; Anna McHugh; Joan Wiseman; Valerie Ingram; Robert Brady, Oliver Plunketts GAA Club; Alan Milton; Niamh Stephenson; Brian Hanratty; Helena Doherty, Sisters of Mercy, Bessbrook, Co. Armagh; Hugo Greene; Aimee Corcoran, Clogher Head lifeboat; Tom Oliver; Joe Woods; the Old Drogheda Society; the staff of the Millmount Museum; the staff of the National Library of Ireland; and my wife Bernadette for all her help, support and patience while I was researching and writing this book.

Left: Laurence's Gate, with two locals posing for the photographer close to a gas lamp supplied from the Drogheda gas works. These opened in 1822 on the north side of the river and then moved to Marsh Road on the southern side in the mid 1800s, eventually closing around 1970. One figure closely associated with Laurence Street was P. L. Cooney, who had a wallpaper and paint shop there for many years. Before the Old Drogheda Society was founded in 1964, he was the person who campaigned for the preservation of the town's past, contributing many articles on the history of Drogheda to local, regional and national newspapers and magazines.

Introduction

Drogheda, on the River Boyne, is one of the most historic towns in Ireland. Today, it has developed into a substantial commuter town with rail and motorway connections to Dublin 50 kilometres to the south. Before the great mid-nineteenth century famine, the town had a population of around 17,000 – a figure that has virtually doubled in the intervening years.

The town was founded by the Danes in 911, although some historians say that the Danes actually arrived nearly a century earlier. After the Anglo-Norman invasion of Ireland in 1169, Drogheda came to rapid prominence; it was given its charter in 1194 and for a time rivalled, if not surpassed, Dublin in importance. Before Trinity College was established in Dublin in 1592, close consideration had been given to setting up Ireland's first university in Drogheda.

For centuries Drogheda was in fact two separate towns, one on each side of the River Boyne, a divide that is still reflected in the ecclesiastical division of the town. The northern part – which used to be called Drogheda-in-Oriel (the old name for Louth) is in the diocese of Armagh, while the southern part is in Meath – the two towns weren't united until 1412, although the diocesan and county 'split' remains.

In the 1640s two sieges shaped the future of the town. During the Confederate rebellion early that decade Drogheda was besieged twice, but those events were surpassed by what Cromwell did in September 1649 when he laid another siege. Close on 4,000 people died, including about 2,800 Royalist soldiers and around 700 civilians, while many of the survivors were deported to the West Indies. Cromwell's barbarity in Drogheda remains vivid in the local folk memory to this day. In 1690 another unforgettable historical event took place with the Battle of the Boyne, which – apart from its major political consequences on the wider European political stage – consolidated Protestant rule in Ireland.

During the eighteenth century, Drogheda began its long road to industrial dominance, initially in the textile industry. The following century saw further expansion with the establishment of the town's shipyard and foundry, as well as its own shipping line which ran regular services to and from Liverpool and, later on, Glasgow. Into the twentieth century new industries came to prominence such as Peter Lyons's bakery, the cement factory (now based at Platin, on the southern outskirts of the town) and Coca-Cola, although during the past four decades around 25 manufacturing firms have closed.

The town has many historic buildings, including the now restored Millmount, whose origins go back to prehistoric times, and prominent churches including St Peter's Catholic church on West Street which is renowned for housing the relics of Saint Oliver Plunkett. One of the town's original seven medieval walls still exists; in the early Middle Ages these enclosed a far larger area than the Dublin city walls, a reflection of the relative importance of the two towns at that stage. In transport, the Boyne railway viaduct is one of the most outstanding examples of nineteenth-century civil engineering in Ireland, while the modern M1 motorway bridge that spans the Boyne near Drogheda is an equally outstanding design. In recent years the town has seen two shopping centres develop, Scotch Hall and the Laurence Town Centre, as well as modern retailing units on its outskirts.

Some stories about Drogheda persist, even though they are untrue, like the one about the railway viaduct being built on bales of wool. Even though Drogheda's flag contains the star and crescent, a remnant of the time of the Crusades (Portsmouth also has the symbol on its flag), the often repeated story about the Sultan of Turkey sending three food ships to Drogheda with relief supplies during the nineteenth-century famine is quite untrue.

Many people regret that parts of the old town, like the Bull Ring and the northern side of James's Street, were destroyed for ill-considered developments. Drogheda has also seen much housing development; from the 1960s onwards many houses were built on the northern fringes of the town, while in more recent years vast housing estates have been built to the south. The town centre itself, including the main West Street, has seen many of its shops close due to the recession, while the major expansion planned for Scotch Hall remains to be completed. But despite these changes, or perhaps because of them, Drogheda retains a strong commitment to preserving its history, which is celebrated here in these pages.

In this photograph, taken early in the twentieth century, a steamship belonging to the Drogheda Steam Packet Company is seen heading for the Boyne Viaduct and the town beyond. One of the most famous trading names associated with the town, the company was set up in 1826. For 76 years it ran a frequent service from Drogheda to Liverpool and Glasgow. In many respects the company was innovative, being the first of its kind to use electric lighting onboard and the first to give third class passengers berths. It lasted until 1902, when it was absorbed into the Lancashire & Yorkshire Railway Company, which in turn was absorbed by the British & Irish Steam Packet Company (itself absorbed into the Irish Continental line in 1992). The path on the right-hand side of the photograph was part of Donor's Green, an area of land reclaimed from the river in 1850 and named after F.J. Donor, the engineer who was in charge of developing the park that was built on it. In the old days of the port, this was an ideal place to watch ships turning in the narrow confines of the river. The area is overgrown and scarcely used nowadays, although there is a campaign in progress to have it restored to its original state.

Before the viaduct at Drogheda was built the railway line from Dublin, opened in 1844, terminated at a station on the south bank of the river, on the site where the train care depot at the present Drogheda Station is located. On the northern side of the river the line from Portadown ended at Newfoundwell, where a collection of sheds and huts formed a makeshift station. Passengers going from one station to the other had to make their own way through Drogheda, crossing St Mary's Bridge which connected the Bull Ring with Shop Street. The viaduct was designed by a Co. Louth-born engineer, Sir John MacNeill. A total of 23 tenders were received and the successful bidder was William Evans from Cambridgeshire, who had built the tubular bridge at Conwy in North Wales. Despite the financial difficulties of the contractor, the viaduct was completed in early 1855 at a cost of £125,000. The clearance above high water is 30 metres. One of the oft-repeated myths about the viaduct was that the piers were built on wool; what really happened was that when cofferdams were built for piers 13 and 14, bales of wool were used to absorb seepage from the river and when the foundations were laid the bales were left in place. In the early 1930s the present lattice-like barriers on the viaduct were built by a Scottish firm, the Motherwell Bridge & Engineering Company. To commemorate the work, the Motherwell company produced special matchboxes which were sold locally.

The North Quay a century ago. The South Quay, seen on the right, was renowned for Grendon's foundry, which at its height in the mid-1800s employed 600 people. It made everything in iron, from farm implements to ships and railway locomotives. It even produced the parts for St Dominick's Bridge in Drogheda and the bridge over the River Boyne near the position of the battle obelisk, but in October 1890 all the implements and machinery of Grendon's were sold by public auction. The Drogheda gas works were near the South Quay; they closed in 1970.

A group of cyclists going along the North Quay in the early 1950s. Cycling remains a popular sport in and around Drogheda, especially with members of the Drogheda Wheelers cycling club. The Central Bar is now the Mariner's Bar, but Greene's sweet and tobacco shop at number 5 is long gone. At the nearby Mall, the old Drogheda Harbour Commissioners (established in 1790 as part of Drogheda Corporation) and more recently the Drogheda Port Company had their offices. In 2009 the port company moved from the Mall to Harbourville on the Mornington Road.

Moving north from the riverside, this photograph shows Laurence's Gate, the last remaining medieval site in Drogheda. It is actually a barbican, meaning that it may have had a drawbridge or a defensive ditch, and it was part of the original town walls which once enclosed an area of 2.5 kilometres in circumference, larger than the town wall of Dublin. The gate was either named after the hospital of St Laurence on the nearby Cord Road, which was probably a leper hospital, or Lord St Lawrence of Howth who was involved in the building of the gate. It was extensively restored about 1700 and a further restoration was completed in 2003. In Laurence Street, on the left-hand side, the elaborate facade in the middle of the row of buildings belongs to the Whitworth Hall, built as a community centre by Benjamin Whitworth, the local MP, at a cost of £4,000 and opened in 1864. It was renowned for its social functions and later housed the Boyne Cinema. Dr T.K. Whitaker, for many years the secretary of the Department of Finance and the man credited with laying the foundations in the 1960s for the start of Ireland's economic progress, lived in Drogheda for much of his childhood. He remembers that cinema matinees in the Whitworth Hall were a special treat – 4d to get in – and he also enjoyed roller skating in the hall. These days its more mundane facilities include pool tables and slot machines. At the extreme left of the photograph is part of the facade of the Drogheda Grammar School, founded in 1699 and closed down in 1979. The school moved to its present premises just outside Drogheda and the original building was demolished in 1989, amid much controversy. One of the distinguished pupils of the school was Henry Grattan, the eighteenth-century MP of the Irish parliament who opposed the union of Ireland and Britain. The elaborate houses on the opposite side of the street, numbers 30, 31 and 32, were built in the mid 1700s for a select few aldermen and burghers of the town, the plasterwork of the façade reflecting the wealth of the original occupants.

Laurence Street has changed much since this photograph was taken in the early 1930s. At that time the building on the left of the photograph belonged to the Provincial Bank of Ireland, one of the banks that merged to form the AIB group. The building was designed by William G. Murray in 1860 and the striking facade is still in place but the building is now used as a branch of the AXA insurance company. A little further up the street from the bank building, but not visible here, is the entrance to the Highlanes Gallery, opened in 2006. This was previously the eighteenth-century Franciscan church (the Franciscans had arrived in Drogheda in 1240), remaining in use until 2000 when it was handed over to the local council and converted into the gallery. It houses the Drogheda art collection and it also displays the 300-year-old mace belonging to the town's corporation.

West Street, looking towards the dome of the Tholsel. This dates from 1770, when it replaced an earlier tholsel. For close on a century, until 1899, it housed the Drogheda Corporation. This then moved to the old corn market and courts in Fair Street, where it is still based. The Tholsel eventually housed a bank, but became derelict. A major restoration programme was completed in 2011 and the building now contains the town's tourist office.

West Street a century ago, long before it was partially pedestrianised as it is today. The tower and spire belong to St Peter's Church. The first church on this site had been consecrated in 1791 and was partly incorporated into the present church, built a century later. It is most famous for having the shrine of St Oliver Plunkett, with relics including his head. He was the Archbishop of Armagh and Primate of All Ireland, and was martyred at Tyburn, London, in 1681. He was canonized in 1975, the first new Irish saint in over 700 years. On the opposite, southern, side of West Street, the oldest business still trading is undoubtedly Kieran's deli and butchers, opened in 1924. Another noted retailer in West Street was Anderson's fashion store, where Ben Dunne served his time. He founded his retailing empire, Dunnes Stores, in Cork in 1944 and one of the earliest stores he opened was in West Street, incorporating Anderson's. A retailing landmark that disappeared in recent years was Schwer's newsagents at the corner of West and Peter streets, replaced by a dull building housing a branch of the Permanent TSB bank. Schwer's building once also housed Kavanagh's bakery. Woolworths is another retailing name to have disappeared from the street. At the top end of West Street the road literally narrows into Narrow West Street (not visible in this view) where many changes have also taken place. The former Drogheda Garda station was situated there in a 1734 townhouse that now accommodates the Droichead Arts Centre.

Opposite: In June 1932 the Eucharistic Congress was staged in Dublin and when it concluded the papal legate, Cardinal Lorenzo Lauri, went on a tour of Ireland. In Co. Louth he stopped off in Dundalk and Drogheda and this photograph shows the grand occasion when he celebrated Mass at St Peter's Church. The elaborate insignia of the Eucharistic Congress can be seen above the main entrance to the church, while below it is the shrine with the relics of St Oliver Plunkett. His beatification in 1920 is still commemorated in early July every year by taking his relics in procession through the town, and the church holds a special Mass in his honour on the last Friday of every month.

This photograph was taken on Sunday, 25 May 1941, outside St Peter's Church during the inauguration of the first Drogheda ambulance unit of the Order of Malta. The ceremony followed the twelve o'clock mass. The two men shaking hands are the Marquis McSwiney of Mashanaglass (facing the camera), the president of the order, and Sergeant B.J. McKenna, the NCO in charge of the new Drogheda unit. To the left of the Marquis is Thomas Gaisford St Lawrence, predecessor of the present chancellor of the order in Ireland, John Graeme Igoe. Also in the photograph, to the right and wearing a homburg hat, is Dr Joseph Hardy, a Drogheda doctor who was medical officer to the new unit.

As early as 1910, when this photograph was taken, the Boyne Valley had become a popular place for tourists. This horsedrawn tour is seen setting off from the offices of the Great Northern Railway in West Street, Drogheda.

The Imperial Hotel in West Street after it was destroyed by fire around 1885. Built in the early 1800s and known as the White Horse by the mid-nineteenth century, it was owned by the Simmcock family and later by the Keappock's. One of the Keappock family members left £14,000 on their death in 1898, equivalent to €1.3 million today. The hotel was listed in local directories as being in a ruinous state between 1886 and 1893. The hotel was resurrected after the fire and, renamed as the White Horse, continued to trade for many years. In 1992 its name was changed to the Westcourt Hotel. Some famous figures had connections with the old White Horse Hotel. John Cassidy, born in Slane in 1860, worked as an apprentice bar tender there and later he became a renowned Manchester-based sculptor. Woodrow Wilson, later the 28th US president, stayed in the White Horse in 1899. So too did the writer C.S. Lewis when he was visiting his brother Warnie in hospital in Drogheda in 1947. During his visit Lewis met Mother Mary Martin, the founder of the Medical Missionaries of Mary in Drogheda. Another fire in West Street burned out the post office on 19 December 1946. It took five years to design and build the replacement post office, also on West Street and, much refurbished, is still in use today. This originally included a telephone exchange, although the first telephone exchange in Drogheda had been opened on the other side of West Street, next to St Peter's Church, in 1893. However, the telephone was slow to catch on and as late as 1934 Drogheda had a mere 120 to 130 telephone subscribers. Some of the earlier switchboards and phones used in Drogheda now form part of a display in the Millmount Museum.

Gray's cycles and motors was a noted fixture in West Street where it funnels into Narrow West Street. It was opened in 1917 by James Gray from Woodstown in Ardee, Co. Louth, and the business also sold hardware, household goods and furniture, as well as carrying out plumbing repairs and some tin-smithing. When Gray died in 1922 his four sons took it over and concentrated on cycle and motor car repairs and sales. The shop closed down in 1982.

A fleet of lorries belonging to Peter Lyons's bakery, pictured in the 1930s in Leland Place, close to the bakery in Stockwell Street on the north side of town. The original Lyons's bakery in Drogheda was run by Thomas Lyons in Trinity Street; this was eventually sold in 1940 to Patrick McCloskey, father of Malachy McCloskey, founder of Boyne Valley Foods. In 1890 Peter Lyons, grandfather of the present Peter J. Lyons, started his own rival shop to Thomas's in West Street. His business prospered and in 1905 he bought a brewery in Stockwell Street and turned it into a bakery. Ironically, the offices of the new bakery had once been the home of the McCloskey family. In the 1920s and '30s, Drogheda had close on a dozen bakeries, including Galbraith's and Tighe's, both of which Peter Lyons bought. By the 1970s Peter Lyons's bakery was employing about 150 people. The shop in West Street, with its ornate interior, was sold in 1975 to what was then the ACC Bank and the building is currently unused. The bakery itself closed in 1986 and part of it became the Drogheda Arts Centre. Today, the main Drogheda library is located in Stockwell Street.

Peter Street, which runs uphill from the Tholsel towards St Peter's Church of Ireland (the tower of which can be seen here in the top right). On the right-hand side of the photograph the parish centre, the large building towards the top of the street with the single window, has been replaced by the Barbican Parish Centre, which includes substantial performance space. It was built as part of the Laurence Town Centre development, a shopping complex that opens onto both Peter Street and Laurence Street. The off licence on the left, at the foot of the street, was run for many years by Joe Egan, who sold it in 2004. His brother Paul, along with Paul's two sons, run the Black Bull pub, restaurant and shop complex on the Dublin Road. Charles Egan, father of Joe and Paul, opened the town's first supermarket in the late 1950s. At the top left-hand side of Peter Street is Clarke's pub, a traditional venue that has changed little in more than a century's trading. The building itself dates back to 1800, with the present-day facade of the pub dating from around 1890. Its first owner was Thomas Reid, whose daughter Nano Reid (1905–1981) was a renowned artist.

The Magdalene Tower in Upper Magdalene Street on the north side of Drogheda is the last remaining portion of a Dominican abbey founded in 1244; the tower itself was built in the fourteenth century. The thatched cottages in the foreground have long since vanished and the tower is now surrounded by a small grassy area and modern houses, while the St John of God centre for people with disabilities is nearby.

Scarlet Street is much changed from when this photograph was taken at Kieran's Corner in the 1930s. The thatched cottage in the centre of the photograph is long gone. The white building on the right was a dairy that sold milk in cans, while the roof of the building just behind the 'Stop' sign was part of a fine house that belonged to Joe Woods, a well-known local cattle dealer.

The building which can be partly seen here on the extreme left was the Drogheda Linen Hall, built in 1774 for linen markets (and it was later used by small linen companies for storing their wares). By the end of the eighteenth century and for much of the nineteenth, Drogheda had a thriving linen trade, but eventually the hall fell into disuse and was demolished in the early 1970s. Murdock's, the noted building supplies firm, had their Abbey Sawmills close by here. While the firm was a substantial timber merchant, it also supplied cement, hardware and ships' supplies from premises on the South Quay, close to the Bull Ring. The elegant church next to the hall is the Dominican church, designed in the French gothic style and built in the 1880s and in front of it can be seen the start of St Dominick's Bridge. The tall spire behind the church belongs to St Peter's in West Street. Behind that, to the left, is St Peter's Church of Ireland in Peter Street, built in 1752. An earlier church on the site sheltered people from Cromwell's attack in 1649. The steeple was set on fire by Cromwellian troops, killing 100 people who had sought refuge there. The interior of the present-day church has beautiful baroque plasterwork but an arson attack in 1999 caused severe damage, although by 2007 an extensive renovation programme had been completed. However, just south of the church two rows of houses built facing each other for the widows of clergy remain derelict.

The old chimney of the Greenmount and Boyne Linen Company at Greenhills. In the 1930s the textile industry was still a substantial employer in the town, with a total of 3,000 people working in two spinning and weaving mills, the Greenmount and Boyne and Robert Usher's. In 1925 the Boyne Weaving Company in Drogheda had been acquired by the Greenmount Weaving Company in Dublin, but the prosperity of the newly amalgamated firm was short lived. The reduction of exports in the 1930s meant a substantial decline in trade for the two mills, which never recovered after the Second World War. Before 1932 the company exported 70 per cent of its products, but by 1939 that figure had fallen to 25 per cent and it became over-dependent on a limited home market. Even in the 1940s the firm still employed over 1,000 people and it remained a major employer in Drogheda until the 1970s.

Overleaf: Christmas festivities for workers at the Greenmount and Boyne Linen Company, probably in the early 1930s when the textile industry in Drogheda was still a substantial employer of around 3,000 people, mostly women. The company was noted for having a very active social club.

Moving south of the river, this is the Bull Ring, photographed around 1903. It was so called because from medieval times until the early 1800s the area was used for bull baiting, in which the bulls were tethered to a stone pillar and baited by bulldogs – a spectacle which attracted huge crowds. Wexford and Birmingham were also famous for their bullrings. This historic part of Drogheda was swept away during road widening in the early 1980s that also saw the demolition of the side of James Street nearest the river. The bypass that was built quickly proved inadequate and these days the M1 motorway runs close by the town. Looking beyond the Bull Ring, across St Mary's Bridge, Shop Street rises up to the cupola-topped Tholsel. One shop that no longer exists in Shop Street is John Collins hardware shop, which was at numbers 32 and 33. It began trading in 1775 and lasted for 200 years, complete with a giant carving knife and fork sign outside the premises. Maurice Collins, who was born over the shop in 1907 was the fifth generation of the family to live above it. He died in 2003, aged 96. Other once familiar shops in the street were the Imco dry cleaning establishment and McNamara's which sold everything from seeds to groceries and animal feeds. The Drogheda Independent, founded in 1884, is still based in the street however, as is Madame Le Worthy's newsagent's shop which has been in business there for nearly a hundred years. Shop Street is also noted for its Augustinian church. The first Augustinian foundation in Drogheda was created in 1295 and the foundation stone of the Shop Street church was laid on 28 September 1860. By the late 1990s the structure of the church had deteriorated so much that substantial reconstruction became essential.

Lochrin's shop in the Bull Ring was in business from the late nineteenth century until the mid 1970s and sold a wide variety of hardware and other items such as toys, including Meccano parts. Its managing director, Owen Lochrin, was one of twelve Irish businessmen killed in the June 1972 air crash at Staines, near Heathrow Airport. They were on their way to Brussels as part of an Irish delegation seeking membership of the then EEC (Ireland became a member on 1 January 1973). Owen Lochrin's mother Mary had died a fortnight before the plane crash; his wife Helen lived until July 2001. All three are buried in the Calvary Cemetery in Drogheda. Other old shops in the Bull Ring included Thomas Daly's bar and grocery on the west side, next door to Tuite's the butcher (formerly Carolan's), while on the opposite side Reynold's sweet shop by the bus stop was always popular with both adult and kids for its terrific array of confectionery.

St Mary's Bridge, which linked the Bull Ring to Shop Street. Opened in 1864, it replaced a bridge from 1722, which itself replaced the first stone bridge here, built in 1636 (there had been a wooden bridge from 1136). St Mary's Bridge in turn was replaced in the mid-1980s by a much more prosaic and characterless construction, part of the town bypass built at the same time. Until this bypass was built, all the through traffic between Dublin and Belfast crossed the river here, using Shop Street and West Street as part of the main route between the two cities. A sign on the derelict site beyond the bridge advertises Greene's furnishing centre and antique gallery, founded in 1886 by Edward Greene, great-grandfather of the present owner, Hugo Greene. For some years, the antiques side of the business was based at Dunany Point on the Co. Louth coast but is now in Dromod, Co. Leitrim. The Greenes were originally from Scotland and, before opening their furnishing store, they ran a flour mill in Drogheda for two centuries.

St Mary's Church in James's Street, built in the Gothic style in the early 1880s. The interior is richly decorated, but the aisle windows are fitted with very dark glass so the only natural light comes from the clerestory windows, making the church interior very gloomy. The organ was built in 1883 by T.W. Magahy of Cork; it was originally designed for a trade fair. The first Mass in the church was celebrated in 1884. The side of James's Street that the church stands on survives largely intact; the other side of the street was swept away in the early 1980s, with the loss of many interesting small shops. These included the sewing machine shop run a great Drogheda character, Seán ó Dugáin who was well known for his sense of humour; he had a notice in his window which read 'old sewing machines repaired – guaranteed to go like a woman's tongue'. He died on 4 March 1964. In the foreground of the photograph is a conglomeration of small streets and houses, still there today, although much changed. Sampson's Lane is in this immediate area; it used to be called Old Cornmarket Hill. A plaque in the lane commemorates Captain Bernard Daly of the 1st Battalion, Dublin Brigade, Old IRA, who gave his life for the Republic on this spot on 26 August 1922.

A view from Buttergate, near John Street, looking towards the northern heights of Drogheda. St John's Gate, as it was officially known, was one of seven gates built as part of the town's defences in the twelfth century and is one of only three that survive (along with Blind Gate and Laurence Gate). Buttergate was possibly so called because farmers may have paid their tolls to enter Drogheda with butter instead of money; other sources say that the name is a corruption of the name of the Bothair gate, which led to the medieval hospital of St John (*Bothair* is Irish for 'road'). In 1959 some of the gate was demolished as it was in a dangerous condition, but a good deal of it still stands. On the skyline to the left can be seen St Peter's Church in West Street, while on the right is St Peter's Anglican church; the Magdalene Tower is between the two. The large building directly in front of Buttergate was the abattoir in John Street. Most of this street was demolished during the building of the inner bypass in the early 1980s.

The ruins of Buttergate, left, with St Dominick's Bridge spanning the river. It was built as a road bridge but is now for pedestrian use only. The Dominican church is to the right of the bridge.

The great Martello tower at Millmount, pictured before its partial destruction by Free State forces in July 1922 during the Civil War. It had been built in 1808 during the Napoleonic Wars, but a mound on this site dated back to prehistoric times. The complex at Millmount also housed army barracks from 1905 until 1922. The tower was partially restored in 1970, a job that was completed by Drogheda Corporation in time for the Millennium celebrations in 2000. All the buildings in the courtyard complex, some dating back to the 1770s, were also restored and now include a museum run by the Old Drogheda Society. From close by Millmount, Pitcher Hill Steps run down to the Bull Ring. A plaque on the steps commemorates Liam Leech of the First Battalion, Ninth Brigade, Old IRA, who was killed by British soldiers on this spot on 26 August 1922. Moira Corcoran and Harry Fairtlough were the two main movers behind the Millmount Museum project. Harry, who had been active in the old IRA from 1918 until 1924, died in December 1984, aged 83, after collapsing with a heart attack at the top of these steps.

The house in this photograph is the eighteenth-century Governor's House, part of the Millmount complex. The structure of the house has changed little and it is now used by the Old Drogheda Society. In the photograph the land behind the wall is barren, but today a profusion of trees grows there.

Competition in the bakery business – a horsedrawn breadcart belonging to Peter Lyons's bakery trots past McCloskey's bakery shop in James Street. McCloskey's still has a bakery shop in Trinity Street and a bakery at Mell, Drogheda, and the Moorland Café in West Street is owned by a member of the McCloskey family. Drogheda is also renowned as the home of Boyne Valley Foods, set up and run by Malachy McCloskey who by 2010 had been at the helm for over 50 years.

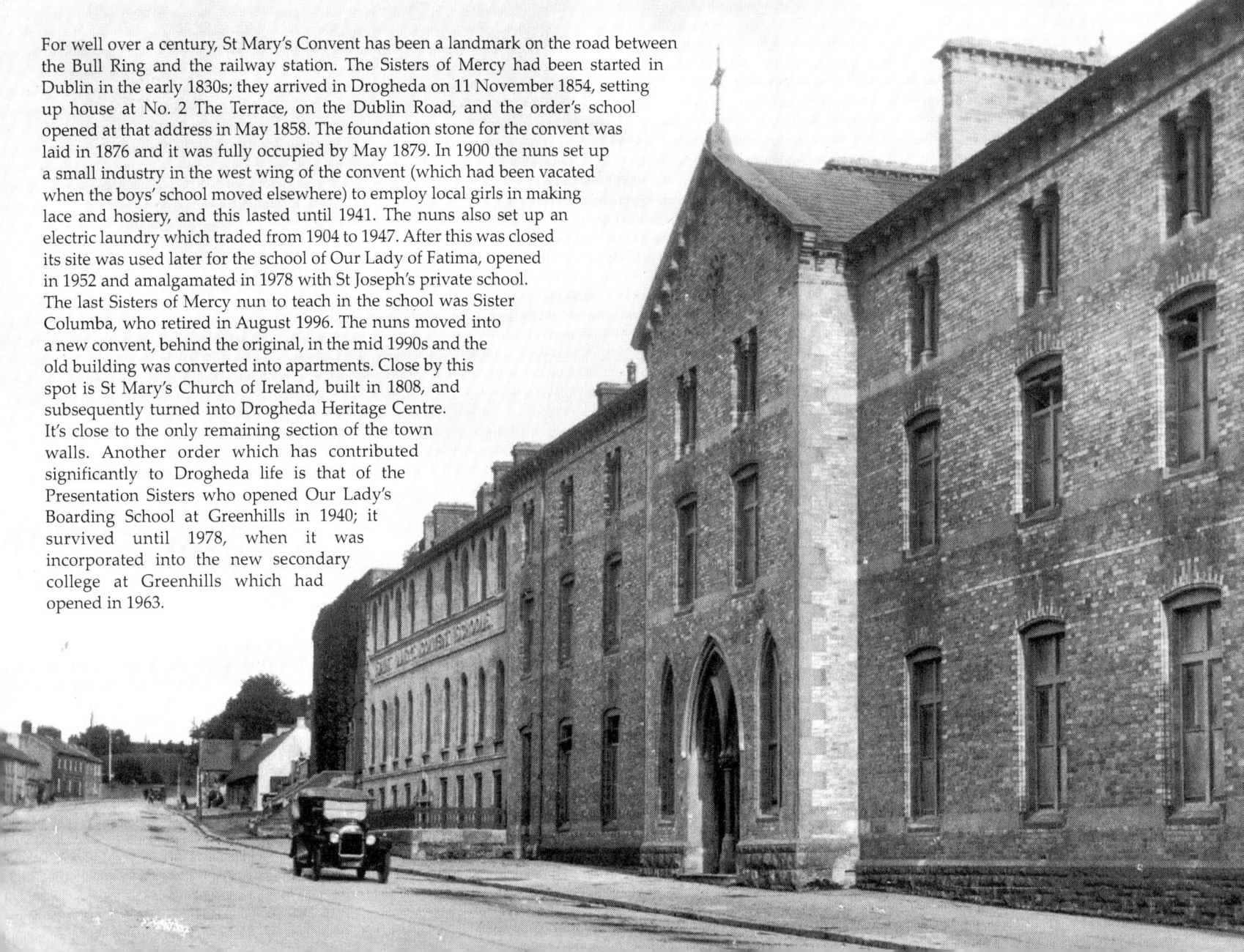

For well over a century, St Mary's Convent has been a landmark on the road between the Bull Ring and the railway station. The Sisters of Mercy had been started in Dublin in the early 1830s; they arrived in Drogheda on 11 November 1854, setting up house at No. 2 The Terrace, on the Dublin Road, and the order's school opened at that address in May 1858. The foundation stone for the convent was laid in 1876 and it was fully occupied by May 1879. In 1900 the nuns set up a small industry in the west wing of the convent (which had been vacated when the boys' school moved elsewhere) to employ local girls in making lace and hosiery, and this lasted until 1941. The nuns also set up an electric laundry which traded from 1904 to 1947. After this was closed its site was used later for the school of Our Lady of Fatima, opened in 1952 and amalgamated in 1978 with St Joseph's private school. The last Sisters of Mercy nun to teach in the school was Sister Columba, who retired in August 1996. The nuns moved into a new convent, behind the original, in the mid 1990s and the old building was converted into apartments. Close by this spot is St Mary's Church of Ireland, built in 1808, and subsequently turned into Drogheda Heritage Centre. It's close to the only remaining section of the town walls. Another order which has contributed significantly to Drogheda life is that of the Presentation Sisters who opened Our Lady's Boarding School at Greenhills in 1940; it survived until 1978, when it was incorporated into the new secondary college at Greenhills which had opened in 1963.

The engine sheds at Drogheda railway station. Today, a substantial depot for cleaning and maintaining trains stands on the site. The original station on the southside of the river was opened in 1844; the site was eventually converted into Buckie's sidings, part of which are seen here. The current station opened in 1855 when the Boyne Viaduct was completed; it was renamed MacBride Station in 1966 when many railway stations were renamed in honour of leaders of the 1916 Easter Rising, in this case Major Tom MacBride. On the northern side of the river the branch line to the then new cement factory at Boyne Road was opened in 1938. For many years an aerial conveyor system, usually referred to as the 'buckets', took limestone for the cement factory across what was the old main Dublin–Belfast road just north of Drogheda. The new cement factory at Platin, south of Drogheda, opened in 1972, complete with its own branch line. From MacBride Station a branch line runs to Tara Mines in Navan and is used to transport ore to Dublin port. At one time the line continued as far as Kells and Oldcastle, but this section was closed down in 1958. In recent years, as Drogheda has become a major commuter town for Dublin, the railway station has assumed even greater importance. During the 1970s, the station was well known for three great 'characters' who worked there – Benny Campbell, Barney Woods, and Barney's wife Kitty, who ran the shop on the main platform for Eason's before taking it over herself. Barney Woods died in 2011.

The Drogheda Chemical Manure company was started in 1867 by F. St George Scott and opened its factory on the Marsh Road eight years later. Eventually, the factory got its own acid plant so that it could make sulphuric acid for its fertilisers. During the Second World War fertilisers were in short supply and the factory had to rely on Ireland's only phosphate mine, located in Co. Clare (phosphoric acid, made from phosphate, is a key ingredient of fertilisers). The company managed to last until 1968, when it was taken over by Gouldings, another big fertiliser maker, but that acquisition was short lived. The site was bought in 1972 for the then new McDonnell's food products factory, which itself is now part of Drogheda's industrial history as it closed in the late 1980s.

The Co. Louth GAA football team, which won the all-Ireland final in 1912. Two years previously they had beaten Kerry in the final. The county had to wait until 1957 for the feat to be repeated. In the 1912 match the Tredaghs GAA Club in Drogheda supplied most of the selection and the match was played at Jones's Road, Dublin. The score was Louth 1-7, Antrim 1-2. One of the players pictured here, Edward Burke, was an ardent nationalist and during the 1916 Easter Rising he was one of a number of men who attacked the RIC station in Ashbourne, Co. Meath. He was captured soon afterwards and when he returned to Drogheda as a prisoner he was greeted by a large and hostile crowd on the Dublin Road. The Easter Rising was far from popular in Drogheda due to the conservative politics of many of its residents. The Tredaghs club, defunct since the late 1920s, also won the junior GAA football championships in 1911 and 1912. In soccer, the original Drogheda United was founded in 1919 and merged with Drogheda FC in 1973 to form the present-day Drogheda United.

Overleaf: Around 50 years ago street leagues were popular in the GAA as a means of getting youngsters interested in Gaelic sports. About 1960 Drogheda had half a dozen of them, including this one from Duleek Street, close to Millmount. This photograph shows the team assembled for a match played in Balbriggan, when it won gold medals for its achievement. Many of the street league games in Drogheda at that time were played at Marian Park, on its then brand new pitch.

Duleek St Under 14, 1960. Game played in Balbriggan. Won Gold Medals.

Back: Dennis Craven, Michael Cavin, Paul O'Brien, Liam Kavanagh, Tony Devin, Paddy Bedford, Peter Lynch, Joe Kelly (Capt), Eddie McGovern

Front: Bobby Murray, Tim Gorman, John McGovern, Joe Leech, Ollie Carolan, Tim Duffy, John Martin, Harry Rooney, Dick Duffy, Joe Larkin, Tony O'Brien, Noel Carolan

The Drogheda Rowing Club was once a great institution of the town, with its races attracting widespread interest. The club was founded in 1864 and closed 99 years later. Its boat house, built on the south side of the River Boyne near the great viaduct in 1867, was sold for a mere £100. The club had staged its first race on the Boyne in 1865 and the Boyne Regatta became an annual social and sporting fixture. This photograph shows the club's Senior Eight in action during the 1927 regatta. Their new boat had been launched that year with the help of a bottle of Champagne and the Army Number One band. Mrs Catherine Cairnes, wife of Lt Col. T.A.E. Cairnes, of the local brewing family, launched the boat and said that she hoped the success of the boat and its crew wouldn't be confined to the River Boyne.

A rare combination of political adversaries in Drogheda, pictured just before the general election on 23 June 1943 when Eamon de Valera, the Taoiseach, spoke in the town on behalf of the Fianna Fáil party which went on to win the election. (Two years before this photograph was taken, Drogheda Fire Brigade had gone to help fight the Blitz fires in Belfast, as part of the southern rescue effort, on the orders of de Valera.) Next to de Valera in this photograph is General Richard Mulcahy, a distinguished figure from the war of independence, who stood unsuccessfully for Fine Gael but was subsequently elected to the Seanad. Fourth from the left is Roddy Connolly, son of James Connolly, a leader of the 1916 Easter Rising. Roddy was elected as a Labour Party TD for Co. Louth. Third from the left is John Callan, who was Fine Gael mayor of Drogheda at the time. He died in 1953, aged 42. The Callan family had been harness makers since about 1890 and for many years ran a shop at Narrow West Street. Before John died, his wife Sheila opened what would now be considered a convenience store on the premises to raise cash for his hospital treatment. In the 1970s the Callans' son, also called John, took over and opened a restaurant and craft shop there, which subsequently became the base for the computer company he founded, Callan Computers. It is still trading in Drogheda, although is no longer owned by John Callan.

Founded in 1142 by Saint Malachy, Mellifont Abbey was one of the most renowned ecclesiastical places in medieval Ireland. It is on the banks of the River Mattock, about ten kilometres northwest of Drogheda. The abbey was thriving by 1170, and by that time had 100 monks and 300 lay brothers. It became the model for the other Cistercian abbeys in Ireland, its style of architecture imported from the abbeys of the same order in France. It was closed in 1559 and eventually a new abbey was built at nearby Collon. This photograph shows part of the abbey close to a thirteenth-century lavabo, where the monks washed their hands before eating. Today, little of the old abbey remains except for this lavabo, together with some Romanesque arches and a fourteenth-century chapter house.

Part of the ruins of Mellifont Abbey.

The Battle of the Boyne took place west of Drogheda on 1 July 1690 in the old Julian calendar, 12 July in today's calendar. King William had a force of 36,000 soldiers, while King James had 25,000 in his Jacobite army. William won the day, securing victory for English and Protestant rule in Ireland. The main combat areas of the battlefield are now clearly marked and the new interpretative centre nearby tells the full story of this most significant battle. The Boyne Obelisk was built in 1736 to commemorate King William's victory. Nearly 40 metres high, it was the tallest man-made structure in Ireland at the time it was built and it was destroyed by Free State forces in 1923, during the civil war. Plans were announced in 2008 for its reconstruction.

The gates on the left-hand side form the entrance to Oldbridge House, while the bridge on the right crosses the Boyne Canal. The Battle Obelisk can be seen on the far right. Oldbridge House dates from the 1740s and was built either by John Coddington or his nephew, Dixie Coddington. It was designed by George Darley, a local mason and architect, who also designed the Tholsel in Drogheda. The house is now the interpretative centre for the Battle of the Boyne site.

Opposite: A group of catering workers at Butlin's holiday camp at Mosney, just south of Drogheda, soon after it opened in July 1948. The woman on the extreme left of the front row is Eileen McLeer Mulcahy, whose father Tom ran a catering firm and a pub-cum-grocery shop on the Chord Road (in those days it was common for pubs and grocery shops to be combined). Later, Eileen ran her own shop and a small bakery on the same road (which is officially spelled as 'Cord', though the informal name is more commonly used). As for Mosney, this was created in the 80 hectares of Ballygarth estate, which was by the sea and the Dublin to Belfast railway line, that Billy Butlin bought for his first holiday camp outside Britain. It opened amid fierce criticism from the Catholic Church, the *Catholic Standard* thundering: 'Holiday camps are an English idea and are alien and undesirable in an Irish Catholic country.' However, visitors soon flocked to Mosney, attracted by the chalets, the dining hall, the amusement arcade, the theatre and the swimming pool. At its peak, it could accommodate 2,800 campers and 4,000 day trippers. To placate the church, Butlin even built a Catholic church in the grounds. In 1982 the camp was sold to Phelim McCloskey, a member of the well-known Drogheda business family, who continued to run Mosney as a holiday camp for nearly 20 years. In 2001 the place was converted into its current use, accommodation for asylum seekers.

Athcairne Castle, sometimes known as Athcarne, is near Duleek and about twelve kilometres southwest of Drogheda. The castle, which was built during the sixteenth century, is on the banks of the Hurley River, a tributary of the River Nanny. In the 1930s most of the land surrounding the castle was acquired by the Land Commission and divided between local farmers. Among the contents of the castle sold at the time were the furs of the last wolves in Ireland and a bed that King William had slept in for a night prior to the Battle of the Boyne. The castle was retained by the Gernon family and its last occupier, until the early 1950s, was James Gernon, who enjoyed regaling local people with tales of his experiences in the Klondike gold rush of the 1890s. After Gernon left, the castle was partially demolished and the remainder fell into ruin. Subsequent attempts to have the castle restored to its former glory have so far failed.

A group of Meath County Council workers using a steam roller on a minor road at Hill of Pass (commonly called just Pass), near Duleek and Bellewstown racecourse southwest of Drogheda. The year was 1924 and included in the group are Pat Markey (ganger), Jack Reid, Kevitt Clark, Barey McGuinness, Pusey Collier, Braskeen Connell, Dadlum Coleman, T. Matthews (on the roller), Mutt Clinton, T. Murray (and son), Kit Gallagher, Ned Heeney, Joe McKenna and T. Downey.

Fishing on the River Boyne, using time-honoured coracles. For long a feature of the river, these boats were probably invented about 2500 BC by the Neolithic people who created Newgrange, one of Europe's finest examples of an ancient passage grave, which is further up the Boyne Valley. Their construction remained unchanged for nearly 4,500 years – an inner nest built from hazel rods with animal hide providing a waterproof outer layer. An example of a coracle can be seen in the Millmount Museum; it was made in 1944, just four years before the use of coracles was banned following the introduction of a ban on the use of nets in freshwater fishing to protect stocks.

At the turn of the twentieth century Termonfeckin, on the coast east of Drogheda, had a population of about 150. It had Catholic and Protestant churches, a parochial house and rectory, as well as a courthouse and an RIC barracks. Separate schools for boys and girls were housed in a single building at Thunderhill. Termonfeckin also had three blacksmiths, a basket weaver, a tailor and two pubs. The street in this photograph – Big Street – housed a seamstress, a cobbler, a nail forge, a small bakery and a laundry. Most of the men in the village worked as farm labourers on the surrounding Brabazon and Smyth estates, at Rath and Newtown respectively. A feature of life in those days was the custom of better off families to take their pony and trap into Drogheda and do enough shopping to last them for three months. What was once the village's Tearman's Hotel became An Grianan, the headquarters of the Irish Countrywomen's Association, and at one time the village was the summer holiday place for the Archbishops of Armagh. On 4 June 1944 a US Air Force plane crash landed on the local beach; the four-man crew escaped uninjured and were treated to a bottle of Jameson whiskey at the home of Bertie and Joan Taylor before being taken to Drogheda. From there they were returned across the border to Northern Ireland.

The lifeboat named 'Charity', which was in service at the old Mornington lifeboat station from 1885 until 1893. The station was opened in 1872 after the loss of a brig from Whitehaven, Cumbria, on the beach at Bettystown in 1871. The Mornington station closed in 1926. The 'Charity' cost £302 to build, funded by a legacy from a Mrs Bradshaw of Reading. During its service at Mornington, it was called out seven times but made no rescues and did not manage to save any lives. The boat was withdrawn and broken up in 1901. The lifeboat station at Baltray, on the northern side of the Boyne Estuary, opened in 1856 and closed in 1899, but the Clogherhead station, opened in 1899, is still a vital part of sea rescue services off the Co. Louth coast.